SEO Secrets, Myths, and Truths to Being Found Online

SEO is one the best and most trusted ways to be found online. It's organic. It's what you put into making your brand stand out.

Copyright © 2016 Becky Livingston

All rights reserved. No part of this book may be reproduced in any form or by an electronic or mechanical means—except in the case of brief quotations embodied in articles or reviews—without written permission from its publisher, except as provided by the United States of America copyright law.

For permission requests, email the author using the subject line "Attention: Permissions Coordinator" at the email address ContactUs@Penheel.com.

Visit the author's website at http://Penheel.com.

Follow Penheel Marketing on social media.

Twitter	Google Plus
Facebook	LinkedIn
Pinterest	YouTube

Second Edition

ISBN-13: 978-1533240903

ISBN-10: 1533240906

CONTENTS

1. From the Author — 5
2. Why is SEO important? — 7
3. 5 Secrets You Need to Know — 13
4. The Myths — 21
5. Buyer Persona — 23
6. Finding Keywords — 31
7. iSpy — 35
8. 8 SEO Tips to Aid in Search Engine Rankings — 41
9. Keyword Phrase Placements — 45
10. Landing Page Tips — 49

FROM THE AUTHOR

In this book, I will share search engine optimization (SEO) secrets, myths, and truths to help your business be found online. In addition, you'll read about some tricks to find out what your competition is doing; the keywords they are using; and more.

Learn how to use SEO on your website, in email campaigns and on images. Plus, you'll receive an SEO template to help you begin finding the right keywords for your business and the process you can implement within days.

The goal of this book is to provide you with the tools you can use to increase search recognition for your brand, including:
- Gaining insight into being found online;
- Hearing the truths and forgetting the myths about SEO;
- Conducting research to find the right keywords for your business; and
- Implementing the keywords once you find them.

In addition, you'll read about other SEO tips, tricks, and techniques you can begin putting in place today to gain search rankings tomorrow.

What are you waiting for? Let's get moving!

WHY SEO IS IMPORTANT

If you're seeking to be found online as an expert, or you desire to have your website, product, or services found online via organic search, SEO is your tool.

SEO is website optimization with "no dough." One way to remember SEO versus search engine marketing (SEM), is the "O" is for organic, optimized, and for no dough. The alliteration alone should help you to remember it.

Technically, however, SEO isn't free. You need to spend time, energy, and resources to ensure you're doing all you can on your website, behind the scenes, to increase search rankings naturally, both on your site and on search engine crawlers.

Over the years, I have heard arguments that a marketing team should focus its effort on SEO versus SEM, and vice versa. Here, I'll share the benefits of each. And, how you can leverage the power of one or both to influence your branding and overall search rankings.

SEO = Website Optimization for no dough! Well, sort of.

Commonalities

In either case, you must define the overall goal. For example, with an SEO goal, it may be to be on the front page of a major search engine for a specific phrase or keyword. In an SEM campaign, it may be to increase subscriptions to your newsletter, or online registrations for a conference.

Both methods use a heavy emphasis on keywords. The difference is, with SEO you do not pay for the keywords. With SEM, you do pay for keywords. In both cases, you may use the same keywords to help drive traffic to landing pages, key product pages, or brand-related pages, such as services, products, or whitepapers.

Another similarity is the quality of the content. In either case, you want to drive your target market toward good content that sits on your site. The better the content, and the more likely your audience is to share it. Plus, the more influence it will have over a brand's organic search results and quality click- thru rates on paid advertising.

Differences

An SEO approach is more of a long-term strategy, which could take months or years to determine the return on investment (ROI). You must create really good content that is written for the target market. Consistent social media posts and efforts toward driving your target audience to your content are required. It could take months and possibly years to create a solid, lead-magnet flow using this method. Understanding the keywords your target market is using is crucial to the success of this effort.

An SEM approach could be a much quicker return on investment. However, you pay for speed. What's needed here is a solid understanding of the search terms and websites on which you want to feature your content. Also, doing research to know what the budget amount should be to get your content on the top search pages is very important. Lastly, the landing page is crucial. You must develop a well-thought out strategy to ensure the user experience is good, because the experience impacts the price you pay and placement for ads.

In either case, you must think about the overall strategy.

Example
"I ran SEM campaigns … to try and get clients but didn't have much success with it. The best keywords just cost a lot of money and in the end it didn't make much sense for us to keep running the campaigns.

We're now focusing on improving our SEO reach starting with long-tail keywords where it's easier to rank.

I think putting constant effort into building a presence through SEO is a must for every business looking to build a customer base on the long term. SEM can be amazing to gather quick leads (if you have a more short-term goal)."~ Aurelie

SEO Strategy Tips

For an SEO strategy, conduct a keyword audit either on your own or with someone that specializes in keyword audits. You may know some of the keywords your audience may look for, but you may not know the best ones or some of the more, well-known terms that are currently being used.

Further, developing quality content can be time consuming. Do you have the in-house staff to create the content needed to attract the audience you want? If not, consider the budget to get the content you need.

Additionally, take a consistent, meticulous approach to sharing that content. It's about demonstrating your expertise among your audience that helps to drive engagement, including commenting, sharing, and liking. This is not a set-it-and-forget-it approach, using the assumption if you create it, they will come. You must plan, at least, a few hours each month to share, comment on, and create content.

Plus, you now need to think of the call to action you want people to take when they consume the content. Should they share it, like it, download it, subscribe to it, post it, etc.? Giving your audience content direction will help them know what they should do with it.

If you don't provide this element, they may simply read it and close the page.

Are you ready?
Are you ready to engage in SEO and SEM efforts for your brand?

In the End
In the end, both SEO and SEM are worth the time, budget, and effort. Remember that doing either, or a combination of both, requires strategy, monitoring, and care. If you're willing to put in the effort, yourself or to hire someone to do it, and it's done well, an uptick in traffic to your website, online store or video channel, sales conversions, or brand awareness should increase -- significantly.

Be realistic about the time, budget, and energy you are willing to put into the effort. The less you put in, the less you'll get out.

Finally, revisiting your keywords at least annually is an often overlooked element of this strategy. Take for example the word "pretzel." It was pretty innocuous before the food industry put a spotlight on it. If you had any type of product or service for which you could leverage that word, it was important to update your SEO to reflect the new term.

In addition, you'd want to adjust the online ad budget to pay for the keyword since it would have increased in cost due to its popularity.

5 SECRETS YOU NEED TO KNOW

We all know that being found on search engines is a great way to increase leads. However, do you know how to do it?

Here are five SEO secrets you should know to help your company's website rank on search engines.

1. Site submit. If your company's website hasn't been submitted to a search engine, you can do this for free on Google, Bing, and Yahoo!. By doing this, the website is then queued to be crawled by the search engine and all its contents indexed.
2. Keep it fresh. Current and updated content makes search engines happy. Consider running news feed and update your blog at least once to twice a month.
3. Let the long-tail wag the dog. Use long-tail search terms, such as "San Francisco French Bakery," versus something generic like "San Francisco Bakery".
4. The devil is in the details. Meta descriptions for pages and blog posts are key when defining search results. Be sure your website pages and blog posts are using them.
5. Keep the user in mind. Developing content for the user rather than the search engine is important. Write the content using words like "we," "us," and "you." An optimized user experience is very influential when it comes to search results.

Following are tips and tricks about each of these secrets.

Site Submit

It's free to submit a website to Google, Yahoo!, and Bing. Simply search for "site submit" and you'll see links to submit to all three. It's fast and easy!

Secret: If the site is not submitted, you are relying on the search engine to find you, which could take months.

Tip: Do this when a new site launches, when a site's been redesigned, or when a major change has been made.

Keep It Fresh

When sites become stale, search engines do not crawl it frequently.

Secret: Having a scrolling news feed (RSS) item on your site helps to keep content fresh and the crawlers interested. You can find them by searching for the topic name and adding "RSS" after it, e.g., manufacturing rss news feed.

Tip: Add new content to the site easily with updated images and blogs.

Long-Tail Keywords

Rather than using generic terms in your website meta data, such as "plumber," use terms like:

- "Bergen County Plumber"
- "Industrial Plumber Northern NJ"
- "NJ Plumber"
- "New Jersey Plumber"
- "Best NJ Residential Plumber"
- "NJ Residential Plumber"

Secret: Keywords can be on website pages, images, headlines, text on a page, and in sub headings.

The more specific you can get, without going crazy, the better the search results will be and the further down the marketing funnel the searcher is.

In this example, the keyword "plumber" is too generic. It would draw millions of search results. However, "Best NJ Residential Plumber" would draw only thousands of hits, and the person searching to that extent would be ready to engage in your services.

> "You may be wondering why anybody would want to target hundreds or thousands of keywords which bring only small traffic. Well, the answer is simply that there is less competition so you can rank on the first page of Google for long-tail keywords far easier than ranking for short-tail keywords." – Marketing Hub

The Devil's In the Details

The majority of websites allow for meta tags. The most important ones to use are:

- <meta Title> is the title of the page. It's what shows up in your website tab, in search engine results as the title of your page, and influences SEO keyword search.
- <meta description> is a one- to two-sentence description about a web page or blog post. It should include the keyword and must be relevant to the page's content. In many cases, when I do an SEO audit, I find people's websites have the same description and title on each page. This is bad form and Google may actually downgrade your ranking and you will pay more for Google AdWords when you buy ad space.
- <meta keywords> is a short list, roughly 1- 20 words or phrases, that are related to the page's content.

For example, the plumber would not be using terms like "electrician, construction supervisor," etc. in his keywords because they don't match what's on the page, nor do they align with his business.

When using keywords that are not on the page, Google may downgrade your site ranking, blacklist you if it becomes a pervasive issue, or increase your ad spend when choosing Google AdWords as a marketing tool.

If you have a WordPress® site, you must install an SEO plugin, like Yoast™, to enter keywords and meta data. If you do not install an SEO plugin your site will be missing a key ingredient to the "getting found online" formula.

If you have a site on Weebly® or Wix®, adding keywords and descriptions may be an "advanced" link on your pages and blogs. Look for that.

If you have a traditional website, this code will have to be entered manually. There are a lot of HTML source code tools you can use to discover how to write the code needed.

Wordpress SEO Yoast Plugin Example

The SEO title is the title of the page or blog post. The slug will be created automatically. The meta description is a sentence about the content. Be sure to use a keyword in this area. It's what shows up on the search results page. Keyword focus is single word or phrase for the content, for example, plumbing tips. On the right sidebar, there is a "tag" area. That is where your short list of keywords and keywords phases would be. Make sure to enter your company brand as a term. If you are also trying to brand a name, be sure to enter it here, e.g., Becky Livingston.

Title Tag Example
Here's how a title tag works. When you add a title tag to a web page or blog post, the information you add in the tag shows up in search results. It shows up because of a few things:
1. The keyword (shown in bold) is in the title.
2. The keyword is in the description (also shown in bold).
3. The keyword was entered in the keywords tag on the site or blog page.

Description Tag Example
Similar to the title tag, the description tag also includes the searcher's keyword, shown here in bold.

It's important to know how to find keywords for your brand and how to use them on pages, posts, images, and more. That is shared later.

Title tags appear in blue.

Descriptions appear in grey, with the keyword in bold.

Writing for the Reader

Search engines prefer the content on pages and in blogs be written for the reader rather than for the search engines.

In the past, people were keyword-stuffing their pages to help increase the SEO ranking. However, Google noticed this happening, and changed its algorithm to focus on human terms, such as "we," "us," "you," "your," "team," "together," etc. Take this into consideration when writing copy for pages or blog posts. Rather than using generic terms like "the business owner;" use terms like "you."

Every little bit helps when you want to be ranked on the first page and when you want to beat your competition. Using words like "you," "we," "your," and other people-like words will not only draw in readers, but also make the engines happy.

Tip!

How to Create Compelling Content that Ranks Well in Search Engines

This free, 27-page eBook, written by Copyblogger founder Brian Clark, provides a step-by-step strategy for creating content that scores links and social sharing. It is highly readable and engaging, and ranks well in search engines.

Find it online at http:// http:// www.copyblogger.com/seo-copywriting/.

THE MYTHS

In 2015, HubSpot® released it's annual top SEO myths for marketers[1]. Below are several that I feel are relevant. There were also some on their list I don't agree with, like there's no need to submit your site to search engines. Well, if you're the little guy, you might want to reconsider that.

1. More links [link building] are better than more content. Having more relevant content is important than building links. However, having good links to others' content is important.
2. Meta descriptions have a huge impact on search ranking. Meta descriptions are not as relevant for search ranking as they used to be; however, they help set you apart from your competition in the search results.
3. IT can handle the SEO. IT staff have a different skill set than helping you to find the right keywords for your business. Work with someone who understands keyword ranking, search, and placement before asking IT to assist in the project.
4. Keyword optimization is all I need! The short of it is, in the future, search engines may not punish people per se for not using keywords, but it will punish those who use too many. Keywords aid in search results and help you to stand out from your competition.
5. My homepage needs a lot of content. Your homepage content should be long enough to clarify who you are, what you do,

---

[1] http://cdn2.hubspot.net/hub/404976/file-2401560048-pdf/SEO_Myths-

where you're located (if you're local), your value proposition, and what visitors should do next.

6. Local SEO doesn't matter. In July 2014, Google released Pigeon – a new algorithm that puts more weight on local search than ever before. It aids in determining local search rankings for businesses.

7. Bad sites linking to me doesn't matter. When a bad site links to yours, it *does* matter to Google search. If poorly developed, inferior, and offensive sites link to yours, you could be penalized in search rankings – and in some cases black listed – for the connection. One way to clean up bad sites linking to yours is to use Google's Disavow tool to test the link. You can find that at

    https://support.google.com/webmasters/answer/2648487?hl=en.

8. Inbound marketing doesn't impact SEO. Inbound marketing and SEO are directly linked. Driving visitors to your site via online marketing and traditional marketing efforts via links aids in search rankings because search engines track the amount of traffic each sites gets per day/hour/minute. This also impacts your AdWords quality score.

BUYER PERSONA

According to this definition from HubSpot, "A buyer persona is a semi-fictional representation of your ideal customer based on market research and real data about your existing customers. When creating your buyer persona(s), consider including customer demographics, behavior patterns, motivations, and goals."[2]

Having a deep understanding of your buyer is crucial to driving the type of content you create, images, text, tip sheets, graphics, etc., to the sales follow-up that works best to engage and retain them.

At its most basic level, a persona helps you to personalize your efforts toward your target market, whether that's one market or several. For example, you might have a Board of Directors, people who buy one type of service or another, webinar attendees, downloaders, etc. Knowing who and how is important to you so you can tailor your message to what you know about each target market.

What is negative persona?

There is also something called a negative persona. Those are the people you want to avoid marketing to. They might be excluded based on age, gender, geographic location, income, and so many

---

[2] 1 http://blog.hubspot.com/marketing/buyer-persona-definition-under-100-sr

other characteristics. They might also include professionals who are too advanced for your product or service, students who are only engaging with your content for research/knowledge, or potential customers who are just too expensive to acquire

Identifying those people is key to avoid spending marketing time and money.

Who are some of the negative personas you should stay away from, e.g., people under the age of 20, people in countries outside the U.S., etc.

_____

_____

_____

Why is buyer persona important?

The buyer persona – those we plan to market our goods and services to – is important to define prior to developing a content marketing strategy. Here, we take things one step further and begin to create content based on a buyer persona(s) and his/their needs and pain points. The goal is to provide information, tips, tools, and more to help reduce their pain points while considering your product or service as a solution.

In the end, you want to know who your buyers are and the type of journey they take as they move through a buying process. To get to the bottom of their buying behavior, you need to understand them fully.

Choosing your social media platform based solely on trends will get you to spend more time and money than you may need. It's important to KNOW where your target audience is and who they are before jumping into any social media efforts. Any good social media or marketing person will ask you who your target audience is before doing any work for you. If he/she does not, that's a red flag.

Before choosing a platform, you must be able to describe your **ideal client or target market(s)**. The more you know about your ideal client, the better off you'll be picking the right social media platform and marketing effort to start with.

Why Create Content?

There are a lot of moving parts to a content strategy, but when you're working alone or with a small staff, it's hard to keep the roles and responsibilities clear as to who is doing what.

Create a content calendar to help keep the machine running and moving like a well-oiled machine. Here is a short list of reasons why most brands develop a content marketing strategy.

- Increase leads to your website at a low cost
- Become a thought leader in your industry
- Build relationships / excite influencers
- Move leads through the sales funnel

Activity #1 – Buyer Persona

Age Range: _____ Male /Female %: _____

Where do they live:
_____

What are their hobbies?
_____

How much money do they make?
_____

Do they have children? If so, how many / How old? _____

Where do they vacation?
_____

Tell us more about your ideal client?
_____
_____
_____
_____

What are your **business objectives and the social media objectives** to support the goals?

Example: Increase new customers by [%] within the next six months (April 2016) within [niche] industry.

- Social Goal: Increase online exposure using social media platform [Name the Platform], to share information and tips about our brand. Post 3x / wk on this platform with engaging content and images and/or video.

_____
_____
_____
_____

What is your **monthly/annual budget** to spend on marketing and social media efforts?

$_____

In order to define where to go for content, as well as to determine the type of content you need to create, you must first know:

1) Where does your buyer/customer get his/her information? Choose all that apply and fill in the "Other" field for other options.

☐ Internet ☐ Email ☐ YouTube ☐ Social Media ☐ Stores ☐ Reading ☐ Radio ☐ T.V. ☐ Newspaper ☐ In-person events ☐ Networking ☐ Other

2) What are the buyer's pain points and challenges about getting a product like yours?

☐ Price ☐ Availability ☐ Access ☐ Convenience

☐ Rate Topic ☐ Other

_____

3) What is your key marketing message when speaking with this persona? For example, we offer a wide range of products we know you'll love. Write a few potential marketing messages for your brand.

_____
_____
_____
_____
_____
_____
_____

Now that you know more about your buyer, think about their journey through the buying process. What steps do they take before actually consuming or buying your product or service?

Here are the buying phases. Create the content associated with each part of the buying phase based on the image below.

WEBSITE VISITOR

75% are looking for information

23% are comparing

2% are ready to take action

1 **Low- to No-Risk Option**
No registration is rquired or regisgtare with email only.

2 **Comparing Option**
Site visitors know their need and are looking for solutions.

3 **Action Option**
These visitors are ready to take action and make contact.

$$ SALE $$

What type of content is usually created for each option?

Low- to No-Risk Option often includes things like:

☐ Blog articles ☐ YouTube videos ☐ Podcasts ☐ Interviews

☐ eBooks ☐ Templates and Tips Sheets ☐ Reports

☐ Whitepapers ☐ Guides and Resources

The Comparing Option includes content such as:

☐ Social Media ☐ Demos ☐ About Us ☐ Testimonials

☐ FAQs ☐ Guarantees ☐ Trials ☐ Webinars ☐ Newsletters

☐ Endorsements ☐ Get a Quote

The final Option—Action—is very important and includes content like: ☐ Contact Us ☐ Inquire ☐ Buy Now

FINDING KEYWORDS

Shhhhhh...it's a secret.

Without the right keywords on your site, searchers, clients, and leads will have a harder time finding you

When it comes to finding keywords for your site, images, copy, description tags, and more, here is a little secret.

Enter the term for which you want to be found; a phrase is best. At the bottom of the search results page, on either Google or Bing, the engine provides a list of phrases that are the most closely related to the one you just searched for. Those phrases are little golden nuggets you can use to add to your keyword phrase list.

In the plumbing example, I found phrases like "licensed plumbers in nj," " residential plumber," and "commercial plumber."

You may have also find terms you would want to add to a negative list, such as salary, resume, and job description, which you would use in AdWords or online buying campaigns. Keep these terms handy (adding them in a spreadsheet is helpful).

Activity:

What are some keywords you would use to describe your product or service? Now put that term or phrase in the search engine and see what related search terms/phrases the search engines suggests. Write the most relevant ones down.

_____

_____

_____

_____

_____

_____

_____

In addition to using a simple search to find keywords for your brand, you should do some more in-depth research to find keywords and phrases that are right for you.

Below are some additional tools you can use to find great keywords, phrases, cost-per-click data, and search volume by month, country, and more. You may need to create a free account with some of these tools, or do a 14- or 30-day trial for free before buying the service.

I recommend leveraging the Google Keywords Planner tool at least, for which you'll need a Gmail email account to access, which is free. Once inside, you can search for terms via a list, or by adding and searching for them one by one.

- Google AdWords keyword planner [adwords.google.com]
- Keyword Tool [keywordtool.io]
- 117 Keyword Research Tool Alternatives to Google [www.smallbusinessideasblog.com/keyword-research-tools]
- Bing keyword research tool [www.bing.com/toolbox/keywords]
- Moz [moz.com]
- SEM Rush [semrush.com]

iSPY

What's your competition doing? What keywords are they using? What kind of ads are they running? If you ever wanted to feel like a clever spy, now might be your chance.

I love a good bit of recon when I'm working on an SEO audit. It helps me to find terms I may not have considered before, to draw together a group of headlines and phrases I may be able to leverage in online ad campaigns or even on websites.

In this section, I talk about a great tool that I often use to discover what other people are doing when it comes to my clients' competition. Though the tool I'm going to share with you may be used for free, if doing keyword recon is something you plan to do often, consider buying the service for more in-depth information.

Let's spy shall we?

<u>iSpionage</u>
It's a great brand name as well as a great tool. You can find it at <u>iSpionage.com</u> and it's offered for free up to the first 10 results, but does require a paid account to access more information.

Here's how it works. You may enter a competitor's URL then choose the country to find data points on Google and Bing/Yahoo! for:

- Page rank
- Their organic competitors
- Organic keyword they use
- Online ads they are running
- Creative for the online ads
- Landing pages associated with online ads
- How much they are paying for cost-per-click campaigns
- Monthly budget spend
- How long ads have been running
- Share of voice in the space, and more.

Now I'm not an expert when it comes to spying on the competition, so this tool has become invaluable to my clients and me. It helps me to see inside the other companies and to learn more about what's working and what's not without me spending a dime.

Plumbing Example

In the plumbing example, my goal was to find out who my client's competition was, as well as what type of keywords they were using, the amount of monthly budget spend they had, and their overall ranking in the space.

Here you can see the closest competitor, based on size, geographic location, and demographic (information I gained from their website), is Ben Franklin Plumbing.

		SEARCH VOLUME: 30/MO	CPC: $29.03	

Nj plumber

Summary | PPC Competitors (32) | SEO Competitors (62) | Ads (69)

Top PPC Competitors in Google | Bing/Yahoo!

Rank	Advertiser	Days Seen	Monthly Budget	Keywords
1	plumbersnearyou.com	245	$109,998	7,631
2	petro.com	356	$36,085	8,226
3	metuchenplumbingcontractor.com	318	$34	137
4	benfranklinplumbingmc.com	274	$140	110
5	angieslist.com	61	$673,011	47,067

Here's what I learned.

They've been advertising for nearly a year. They have approximately 110 keywords they leverage in online ads, including single terms as well as phrases. They are willing to spend $140 monthly on ad buying.

So how does all this benefit me as I consider keywords from my site?

When I click on the 110 keywords shown here, I am brought to another screen that identifies the term or phrase they are using in online ads.

EXPORT								Results 1 to 50 of 110 1 2 3
☐ Keyword	Ads	KEI	CPC ($)	Average Search Volume	Average Position	Days Seen	First Seen	Last Seen
☐ plumbing in nj	6	91.62	25.79	20	3	357	5/1/2015	4/21/2016
☐ plumber somerset nj	4	85.09	26.72	20	7	199	10/9/2015	4/24/2016
☐ n j plumbing	6	81.74	29.48	40	2	310	6/1/2015	4/5/2016
☐ nj plumbers	5	77.12	27.75	70	3	281	6/24/2015	3/30/2016
☐ plumbers in monmouth county nj	4	75.91	3.99	30	7	352	4/23/2015	4/8/2016

Plus, I can click on the "Other Keywords" number to actually see the words! If those words work for you too, then by all means, use them!

From that screen (shown on the next page), I can also see how they write their text ads. Even though I cannot duplicate the text ads, I can review them for phrases I do like. Then I leverage that information when I'm creating my own ads.

Now, I haven't talked about landing pages in detail yet. They are pages on your website that draw in visitors to interact with your brand in ways such as completing a form, watching a video, playing a podcast, downloading a document, registering for an event, etc.

With this tool, you'll see what your competitors' landing pages look like and how you can create pages that work. And in some cases, you'll also see ones that don't work due to poor design or because they link to a generic page on the website rather than a lead magnet page that collects information from the visitor.

Ad Copy	AEI	Destination Url	Group That Triggers The Ad	Monthly Traffic To This Ad	Avg Rank	Days Seen	First Seen	Last Seen
Plumbers Marlboro NJ - benfranklinplumbingmc.com www.benfranklinplumbingmc.com/ 24/7 Professional Plumbing Services In Monmouth & Middlesex Cty. Call!	64.24	http://www.benfranklinplumbing mc.com/general_plumbing.html	12	70	2.1	104	12/14/2015	3/26/2016
Plumber Morganville NJ - benfranklinplumbingmc.com www.benfranklinplumbingmc.com/ 24/7 Professional Plumbing Services In Monmouth & Middlesex Cty. Call!	55.67	http://labs.natpal.com/lpr?c=3 1381392...	4	110	2.6	103	12/1/2015	3/12/2016
Plumbing Freehold NJ www.benfranklinplumbingmc.com/ 24/7 Professional Plumbing Services In Monmouth & Middlesex Cty. Call!	54.46	http://www.benfranklinplumbing mc.com/general_plumbing.html	1	20	5.4	91	12/18/2015	3/17/2016
Plumbers Marlboro NJ www.benfranklinplumbingmc.com/ 24/7 Professional Plumbing Services In Monmouth & Middlesex Cty. Call!	54.35	http://www.benfranklinplumbing mc.com/general_plumbing.html	15	130	4.8	104	12/18/2015	3/30/2016
Plumber Freehold NJ www.benfranklinplumbingmc.com/ 24/7 Professional Plumbing Services In Monmouth & Middlesex Cty. Call!	52.4	http://www.benfranklinplumbing mc.com/general_plumbing.html	1	50	5.5	69	1/20/2016	3/28/2016

You can also click on the landing page link for those ads to see what it looks like (to emulate if done well).

This sort of research not only aids in on-page SEO, but also aids in online ad buying for text ads, Facebook ads, LinkedIn sponsored posts, and more.

Activity:

Do some research on the keywords for your site/brand/product, using Google or Bing search, or iSpionage.

1. Write down your search term.
2. Write down the alternatives presented that you think makes sense.
3. Circle the ones that you like the most and plan to implement into your site and marketing efforts.

_____

_____

8 SEO TIPS TO AID IN SEARCH ENGINE RANKINGS

There are many factors taken into account for websites to appear in web search results, including:

- The number of sites linking to your site
- Site content
- The number of updates made to the site index
- Algorithm changes
- Site updates to current platform technology

What SEO steps do you need to take to positively influence your site's ranking?

Here are several:

1. Include relevant keywords within the text on the page. Relevant keywords are terms people use to search for the content you're providing. Unsure what those terms might be? Use applications like Google AdWords Keyword tool, or simply search for the content in a browser and look to the bottom of the page for additional search terms and phrases. There are more advanced methods and tools, such as Moz.com and SEOTools.com.
2. Create a clear hierarchy within the site structure. Many SEO professionals talk about a four-step process, where no page is more than four levels from the home page. For example, if you have a Services page, it should be one level from Home. The sub services pages, such as Tax, Audit, Part-Time CEO, etc.

would be two levels from the home page, e.g., Home >> Services >> Tax or Home >> Services >> Audit.

3. Link to relevant and respected websites. It makes sense that search engines give better ranking to sites that link to those with established rankings. For example, rather than connecting to GenericAccountingFirm.com blog article, you'd want to link to respected sites that have good rankings, such as JournalOfAccountancy.com, IRS.gov, AICPA.org, etc.

4. Page load speed also impacts search rankings. If your website has a slow load speed, search engines may downgrade it in the search rankings. Slower sites rank lower on the search scale. To test your site, use a tool like Page Speed Tools, tools.pingdom.com/, or www.webpagetest.org/.

5. Information-rich sites that use the proper "title," "meta," and "alt" attributes help to increase rankings. Let's say you create a blog titled "5 Ways to Avoid Getting Audited." When the page is being created, be sure the "title" tag for the blog includes the term "audit" or phrase "avoid getting audited." Also, in the description for the blog, include a sentence (not a series of keywords) about the page's content, e.g., "This blog post includes five tips to help you avoid an audit." Note, the keyword "audit" is used again. Lastly, if an image is used on this page, the file name for the image should include the word audit, e.g., "Avoid-Getting-Audited.png".

6. Mobile sites are increasing in rankings. If your firm's website is not ready for mobile prime time, now is the time to include this in your strategy. Mobile sites are ranking higher than non-

mobile-friendly sites on smart devices, such as tablets and mobile phones. If your audience is primarily mobile and tablet users, a mobile website is a priority.

7. Page URLs also play a great role in search engine optimization and ranking. If your firm's website pages look something like this "firmname.com/pageid=1857" consider changing it to reflect the page title, such as "www.firmname.com/5-ways-to-avoid-getting-audited" to help increase rankings. Keep in mind that shorter URLs are better than longer ones. Also, remember to use hyphens (-) instead of spaces (%20) in page URLs.

8. URL length is important. Most search engines recommend a 70-character URL maximum. When a search is conducted, the results will display URLs up to 70 characters. Anything beyond that will display with an ellipse (…). This can be tricky and sometimes embarrassing if the last word in the character limited is truncated to form another unsavory term.

Best Practice: On-Page Optimization

Including one or several of these elements on each of your web pages is considered a best practice for many SEO professionals. Include the keyword or keyword phrase:

- At least once in the title tag
- In a header (H1, H2, H3…) tag on the page
- At least once in bold, using a <strong> or <b> tag to define it as bold text
- In the image "alt" tag, which is the description of the image when hovered by a cursor

- In the page URL
- In the meta description for the page

It's more important than ever to pay attention to search engine optimization as mobile and tablet devices begin to increase in use.

How are you optimizing your site for the future?

_____
_____
_____
_____
_____
_____
_____
_____
_____
_____
_____
_____
_____
_____
_____
_____
_____

KEYWORD PHRASE PLACEMENTS

Client question: "When I search for a phrase for my business, my results are on page three. How do I get my company to be on page one?"

Answer: Keyword Usage

When using keywords as part of a marketing effort, choose only 1-3 terms for which you want the business to be known. The more keywords for which you want to be found, the thinner the results, which causes your company to be further and further back on the search results pages.

For example, if you wanted your business to be known as the "Small Business Resource," you would use that keyword phrase in everything, including email, website pages, social media hashtags, online ads, video descriptions, etc.

If your competition is already using it and has a saturation point for that term, find another.

Keyword Placement Tips
1. Webpage description meta field would include that phrase and others on all pages.
2. Webpage keyword meta field would include that phrase on all pages.
3. Email campaigns would have that phrase listed somewhere in it.

4. All staff emails would have that in the signature line.
5. Any images related to business would include the phrase, e.g., file name "woman smiling_Small Business Resource.png".
6. Social media posts would always have this mentioned #SmallBusinessResource as one of the hashtags. This would be used on all social media efforts, no matter what platform.
7. Online ads would use the phrase in some way. See the text and graphical ad samples below. The graphical ad would use the keyword or phrase in the image title, e.g., Be-A-Success-Story_brand.jpg.

Example: Online Text and Graphical Ads

	Keywords	Ad Variation I		Ad Variation II	
1	Keywords	Ad Variation I		Ad Variation II	
2	Campaign - NJ				
3	AdGroup - Interior Design				
4	interior design				
5	interior designer bergen county	Don't Miss Winter Sale	22	60% Off Sale	12
6	interior design bergen county nj	www.MyBusiness.com/WinterSale	29	www.MyBusiness.com/WinterSale	29
7	interior design bergen county new jersey	60% Off already reduced prices.	32	Warm up with these winter prices.	33
8	interior designer paterson nj	Stop in today for the savings.	31	All locations! Stop by today.	29
9	interior designer paterson new jersey				
10	interior designer ridgewood nj	Stop By Today - SALE	20	Online + In-Store Sale	22
11	interior designer ridgewood new jersey	www.MyBusiness.com/WinterSale	29	www.MyBusiness.com/WinterSale	29
12	interior designer morristown nj	Winter sale in progress thru 1/30.	35	Winter prices to warm your wallet.	35
13	interior designer morristown new jersey	All locations. Shop online too.	31	Up to 60% off. 3 Locations	27
14	interior designer ridgewood				
15	interior designer paterson				

BE A SUCCESS STORY!

www.MyBusiness.com   Ads by Google

The more a term is used, the more a company will become known for it. By diluting the phrases and using too many, it's too hard to be known for many things on a search engine. The first step is to determine 1-3 terms for which you want to be known for and then hammer those phrases into every marketing effort.

What are your keywords and phrases that you want to be known for online? Jot down several, then circle the ones that really *are* what you want to be found for.

_____
_____
_____
_____
_____
_____
_____
_____
_____
_____
_____
_____
_____
_____
_____
_____
_____
_____

LANDING PAGE TIPS

Landing pages are critical to any good inbound marketing effort.

There are many elements to a good landing page, but to make them effective and to increase conversions takes more than just great layout. Here are eight tips you can use to create landing pages:

1. Clear, concise, compelling headlines
2. 2-3 sentences about the offer/value
3. 3-5 bullet points about the benefit(s)
4. Form with 3-7 relevant fields
5. Easy-to-notice call to action
6. Relevant or compelling image
7. Social sharing buttons
8. On "submit," directs to a thank you page

Landing Page Elements
- Logo
- Headline
- Image
- Benefits
- Form fields
- Call to Action

In this example, you can see the page is very clean with a minimal amount of copy. When creating landing pages, whether on your website or sales site, e.g., Etsy, keep the distractions to a minimum. Avoid the visitor from seeing content that may take them away from the action you want him/her to complete.

That means removing side bars, blog lists, search features, etc. on a website, and/or creating a search-results page for just the product line the visitors wants to see, e.g., the visitor clicked on an add for lawnmowers. The search-results page should just have mowers on it.

LOGO

Headline: Matches what was clicked.
Subhead provides additional information.

Image or video related to the content.

Short paragraph with supporting information. Keep this to two to three sentences.

1. First feature written in the form of a benefit.
2. Second feature written in the form of a benefit.
3. Third feature written in the form of a benefit.

Optional: Customer testimonial works well here to demonstrate social proof.

Form Headline

Short paragraph clarifies the purpose of the form, and what you're giving in exchange for the personal data.

Name

Email

What problem do you need help solving?

Call to Action

Read our Privacy Policy.

Notes:

MORE ABOUT BECKY LIVINGSTON AND PENHEEL MARKETING

Becky Livingston has over twenty-five years' experience in marketing and technology in financial services and engineering firms. She is the President and CEO of Penheel Marketing. In addition to being a marketing practitioner, Becky is also an adjunct professor, author, and speaker. With a graduate degree from Pace University in Information Systems, Becky also holds undergraduate degrees from two other colleges and also has a Certificate in Corporate Training from NYU. She is also an active member of the Association for Accounting Marketing (AAM).

If you have questions about how to strategize, implement, measure, or report on any of the elements within the book, feel free to reach out to me. Also, if you would like a trainer for your team or speaker at an event, I may be reached at the following contact points:

Email: Becky@Penheel.com
Website: http://Penheel.com
Twitter: @Penheel
Phone: 201-785-7840

Penheel Marketing is a marketing firm that specializes in social media and digital marketing for CPAs and small- to medium-sized businesses. In addition to strategic consulting, the firm provides marketing services, such as content development, blog writing, online advertising, website development, graphic design, copywriting and ghost writing, traditional marketing services, like print ad development, inbound marketing, search engine optimization, and more. Visit the Penheel Marketing website at http://Penheel.com, and connect with us on Facebook, LinkedIn, Google Plus, Pinterest, and YouTube for marketing tips for your firm.

Published Books

The Accountant's Social Media Handbook

SEO Secrets Myths and Truths to Being Found Online

Published Articles

Too numerous to mention, but contributing author for:

AICPA CPA Client Bulletin

AICPA Resource Guide Marketing Tip

CPA Practice Advisor blog

PR New Media Training Guidebook

Growth Strategies 2014 editor and article contributor

InSource *2012 In-House Creative Services Industry Report*

Harvard Business Review *Reinventing Your personal Brand*

Accelerate: The Magazine editor and article contributor

Adjunct Professor

Bergen Community College, New Jersey

Westchester Community College, New York

Need A Speaker

Becky speaks at a variety of business organizations and conferences throughout the year. See her speaking engagement list at http://Penheel.com/Speaking-Engagements.

RESOURCES

- Vital Social Media Marketing Statistics & Insights for 2014 Campaigns
  http://www.mashbout.com/social-media-marketing-statistics-2014/
- Social Media Marketing Industry Report 2014
  http://www.socialmediaexaminer.com/report/
- The Top 10 Benefits Of Social Media Marketing
  http://www.forbes.com/sites/jaysondemers/2014/08/11/the-top-10-benefits-of-social-media-marketing/
- The 30 Most Brilliant Social Media Campaigns of 2014 (So Far)
  http://www.exacttarget.com/blog/the-30-most-brilliant-social-media-campaigns-of-2014-so-far/
- How to Design a Social Media Campaign
  http://www.socialmediaexaminer.com/social-media-campaign-elements/
- 5 Clever Social Media Marketing Campaigns that Went Viral
  http://www.jeffbullas.com/2014/07/15/5-clever-social-media-marketing-campaigns-that-went-viral/#j0fkYvJjWxWkgexC.99
- Demographics of key social networking platforms
  http://www.pewinternet.org/2013/12/30/demographics-of-key-social-networking-platforms/
- Taco Bell Goes Black http://adage.com/article/digital/taco-bell-launches-mobile-app-blacks-social-sites/295604/
- Tumblr Queues Up Autoplay Video Ads to Hit $100 Million Revenue Mark
  http://adage.com/article/digital/tumblr-queues-autoplay-video-ads/295582/
- Tips for Advertisers – How to be successful using Custom Content
  https://advertising.aol.com/blog/tips-advertisers-%E2%80%93-how-be-successful-using-custom-content
- Social Media response flow chart
  http://www.conceptdraw.com/samples/resource/images/solutions/marketing-&-sale-diagrams/MARKETING-AND-SALE-DIAGRAMS-Social-Media-Response-Online-Store-Social-Media-Response-Flowchart.png
- Marketo's organizing content http://blog.marketo.com/wp-content/uploads/2013/11/Organizing-content.png
- Work with James Wehner flowchart http://workwithjameswehner.com/wp-content/uploads/2010/06/mlsp_diagram.jpg
- Attract, convert…image http://www.byhisdesign.com/images/layout/inbound-method.jpg
- 5 Tips for Running Successful Social Media Campaigns
  http://www.socialmediaexaminer.com/successful-social-media-campaigns/
- Instagram Pinterest Example http://www.smartinsights.com/social-media-marketing/social-media-platforms/an-example-of-instagram-and-pinterest-awareness-campaigns/
- How to Use Google+ for Social Media Contests
  http://www.socialmediaexaminer.com/google-plus-post-ads/
- How to Format Posts on Google Plus to Maximize Shareability [video]
  https://www.youtube.com/watch?v=toG5x7E2zjk#t=20
- Content Marketing: The Game
  https://www.pinterest.com/pin/219550550560791491/

www.ingramcontent.com/pod-product-compliance
Lightning Source LLC
Chambersburg PA
CBHW040856180526
45159CB00001B/440